TO:

Geneva

FROM:

Bill & Becky

DATE:

Dec. 23 - 07

ISBN 159449316-2

Just Think

by

Roy Lessin

Just think,

you're here not by chance,
but by God's choosing.

His hand formed you
and made you the person you are.

He compares you to no one else—
you are one of a kind.

You lack nothing that
His grace can't give you.

He has allowed you to be here
at this time in history
to fulfill His special purpose
for this generation.

ROY LESSIN

Just think,
you're here
not by chance,
but by God's
choosing.

"*Thy hands have made me
and fashioned me:
give me understanding,
that I may learn
Thy commandments.*"

PSALM 119:73 KJV

Some people would have us believe that the universe and everything in it happened by chance. The Bible tells us that the universe was formed by our Creator God. Everything that God created was for a purpose— nothing is here by random selection or by unpredictable chance.

What could be sweeter or dearer than to know that no one is nearer to your heart, your soul, or your deepest desires than the One who created you? His caring eyes are upon you, His protecting hands are over you, and His assuring voice says to you, "I have made you. You are Mine."

What an incredible journey Jesus made; what an overwhelming expression of love He expressed; what an awesome purpose He had in mind. When He became a man on earth, He was seeking you; when He stretched out His hands upon the cross, He was reaching out to you. You are the sheep He has come to shepherd. You are the one He calls His own.

PERSONAL
REFLECTIONS

*W*hy is it important

to know that God

created you and that

you are not here

by chance?

Additional Scripture *to* Reflect Upon

*"Then God said, 'Let Us make man in Our image,
according to Our likeness; let them have
dominion over the fish of the sea, over the birds of
the air, and over the cattle, over all the earth and
over every creeping thing that creeps on the earth.'
So God created man in His own image; in the image
of God He created him; male and female He created
them. Then God blessed them, and God said to them,
'Be fruitful and multiply; fill the earth and subdue it;
have dominion over the fish of the sea, over the birds
of the air, and over every living thing that moves on
the earth.' …Then God saw everything that He had
made, and indeed it was very good. So the evening
and the morning were the sixth day."*

From GENESIS 1 & 2 NKJV

*"Thus says the Lord, your Redeemer, And He
who formed you from the womb: 'I am
the Lord, who makes all things, Who stretches out
the heavens all alone, Who spreads
abroad the earth by Myself.' "*

ISAIAH 44:24 NKJV

*"All things were made through Him, and without
Him nothing was made that was made."*

JOHN 1:3 NKJV

His hand
formed you
and made you
the person
you are.

"…All the days

ordained for me

were written

in Your book

before one of them

came to be."

PSALM 139:16 NIV

God's Word says that when
a child is conceived, God is
present, forming the life of that
child. He has been involved in
your life from its very beginning.
Long before you knew your
mother's loving touch, God was
there in perfect love watching
over you.

There is never a time when you are not in His thoughts, close to His side, and near to His heart. His presence in your life is not a small thing or a big thing—it is everything.

In His great generosity,
God has given to you freely,
bountifully, and joyfully. He has
given you the finest, the highest,
the deepest, and the fullest
measure of His love. All that He
has given He will continue to
give to you all the days of
your life.

PERSONAL
REFLECTIONS

*W*hy do you feel

more valuable

knowing that

God formed you?

Additional Scripture *to* Reflect Upon

"*I will praise You, for I am fearfully and wonderfully made; Marvelous are Your works, And that my soul knows very well. My frame was not hidden from You, When I was made in secret, And skillfully wrought in the lowest parts of the earth. Your eyes saw my substance, being yet unformed. And in Your book they all were written, The days fashioned for me, When as yet there were none of them. How precious also are Your thoughts to me, O God! How great is the sum of them! If I should count them, they would be more in number than the sand; When I awake, I am still with You.*"

PSALM 139:14-18 NKJV

He compares
you to no
one else—
you are one
of a kind.

" 'The Lord your God
is with you, He is
mighty to save.
He will take great
delight in you....' "

ZEPHANIAH 3:17 NIV

God is the source of all
creativity. He made only one
"you." He didn't use a mold to
form you–He used His hands,
and He will never use His hands
in exactly the same way again.
The plans God has for you and
the things He will do through
you will never be duplicated.

God was the One who formed you, gave you the breath of life, and brought you into the world. He did this so that His arms could embrace you and His love could keep you. He loves you completely. You never need to earn His love. There has never been a time when you were without His love.

God knows you best, and He
knows best how to fulfill His
purpose and plan for your life.
He will not fail you. As you look
to Him, always remember that
He is looking out for you. You
can be assured that above you
are His tender mercies, around
you is His unfailing love, and
underneath you are His
everlasting arms.

PERSONAL
REFLECTIONS

*W*hy is it important

to understand

and appreciate

your uniqueness?

Additional Scripture *to* Reflect Upon

"Having then gifts differing according to
the grace that is given to us, let us use them...."
ROMANS 12:6 NKJV

"But now, O Lord, You are our Father;
We are the clay, and You our potter; And
all we are the work of Your hand."
ISAIAH 64:8 NKJV

"...There is one God, the Father, of whom
are all things, and we for Him; and one
Lord Jesus Christ, through whom are
all things, and through whom we live."
I CORINTHIANS 8:6 NKJV

"Just as our bodies have many parts and each
part has a special function, so it is with Christ's
body. We are all parts of His one body, and each
of us has different work to do. And since we are
all one body in Christ, we belong to each other,
and each of us needs all the others."
ROMANS 12:4-5 NLT

" 'I am my beloved's, And my beloved is mine....' "
SONG OF SOLOMON 6:3 NKJV

You lack
nothing that
His grace
can't give
you.

"God is able to make
all grace abound
toward you; that ye,
always having
all sufficiency
in all things, may
abound to every
good work."

II CORINTHIANS 9:8 KJV

When God made you, He didn't expect you to make it through life on your own. He made you to know Him, to enjoy Him, and to look to Him for all you need. He didn't make you for failure or defeat. He wants to live His life in you—a life of righteousness, peace, and joy.

Through grace, God will give to you over and over again. Because His supply is abundant, you will never be without; because His heart is full, you will never be empty; because His resources are endless, you will never lack any good thing.

The greatest thing your heart can experience is God's presence. He is greater than any of His gifts, more enjoyable than any of His blessings, and more satisfying than any of His provisions. When He gives Himself to you, there is nothing higher that He can give.

PERSONAL
REFLECTIONS

*W*hy is it
important for you
to understand
the meaning
of grace?

Additional Scripture *to* Reflect Upon

"...It is good that the heart
be established by grace...."
HEBREWS 13:9 NKJV

"Let us therefore come boldly to the throne
of grace, that we may obtain mercy and
find grace to help in time of need."
HEBREWS 4:16 NKJV

"...Be strong in the grace that is in Christ Jesus."
II TIMOTHY 2:1 NKJV

"To each one of us grace was given
according to the measure of Christ's gift."
EPHESIANS 4:7 NKJV

"He said to me, 'My grace is sufficient for you, for
My strength is made perfect in weakness.' Therefore
most gladly I will rather boast in my infirmities,
that the power of Christ may rest upon me."
II CORINTHIANS 12:9 NKJV

"...Those who receive abundance of grace and
of the gift of righteousness will reign in life
through the One, Jesus Christ."
ROMANS 5:17 NKJV

He has
allowed you
to be here
at this time
in history.

"*To every thing
there is a season,
and a time
to every purpose
under the heaven.*"

ECCLESIASTES 3:1 KJV

There is no reason to wish you had been born at a different time in history. You were born at the perfect time. God didn't make any mistakes concerning you.

The Lord's ways are beautiful, and everything He does in you and through you will be a beautiful work.

God is almighty and He will bring to pass His purposes for your life. God has everything that is needed to see that it is done. He will do it perfectly, in the perfect way, at the perfect time.

PERSONAL
REFLECTIONS

*W*hy is it
important
for you to wait
for God's time
and to trust
His timing?

Additional Scripture *to* Reflect Upon

"But as for me, I trust in You, O Lord; I say
'You are my God.' My times are in Your hand…."
PSALM 31:14-15 NKJV

" 'As for God, His way is perfect;
The Word of the Lord is proven;
He is a shield to all who trust in Him.' "
II SAMUEL 22:31 NKJV

"He has made everything beautiful in its time…."
ECCLESIASTES 3:11 NKJV

"When the right time came, God sent His Son…."
GALATIANS 4:4 NLT

He wants you to
fulfill His special
purpose for
this generation.

*"One generation
will commend Your works
to another; they will tell
of Your mighty acts."*

PSALM 145:4 NIV

God has a purpose for your life. Everything you do has significance. God wants to work through your hands, speak through your voice, and love through your heart. He will bless you and make you a blessing to others as you seek to glorify Him in all you are and all you do.

He will guide you into all that is best for you and into all that will take you to the highest expressions of His love. He will lead you by His way, by His words, and by His will. He will guide you down the paths that lead you straight to His heart.

Always remember, when God made you He did so with a purpose and a plan. His hand has remained upon you to this very day. He calls you by name. You are His beloved child…the apple of His eye…the delight of His heart. Today you are in the exact place He wants you to be, and tomorrow He will be with you as He has always been–in goodness, in kindness, in faithfulness, in love.

PERSONAL
REFLECTIONS

*A*re you open

to the ways

God wants to

use you in your

generation?

Additional Scripture to Reflect Upon

*"Whatever I am now, it is all because
God poured out His special favor on me—
and not without results. For I have worked
harder than all the other apostles, yet it
was not I but God who was working
through me by His grace."*
I CORINTHIANS 15:10 NLT

*"God is working in you, giving you
the desire to obey Him and the power
to do what pleases Him."*
PHILIPPIANS 2:13 NLT

*"…Whatever you do, you must do
all for the glory of God."*
I CORINTHIANS 10:31 NLT

*"We are God's masterpiece. He has created
us anew in Christ Jesus, so that we can do
the good things He planned for us long ago."*
EPHESIANS 2:10 NLT

NOTES